A DIFFERENT SHADE FOR EACH PERSON READING THE STORY

CHRISTINE HUME

[PANK]BOOKS

First Edition
1 2 3 4 5 6 7 8 9

Cover photo by Juna Hume Clark
Interior design by Jojo Rita

Library of Congress Cataloging-in-Publication Data

ISBN 978-1-948587-13-6

PANK Magazine
PANK Books

To purchase multiple copies or book events, readings and author signings contact awesome@pankmagazine.com.

A DIFFERENT SHADE FOR EACH PERSON READING THE STORY

after Karlheinz Shockhausen's Hymnen *and*
David Hume's "missing shade of blue"

Imagine if your version of red was much redder and more vivid than somebody else's version of red. It's like we get to see the red of the world in a totally different way. And our lives interact with everything that goes on in a very special and specific way that makes us exceptional or gives us the possibility to be exceptional.—*Brad Falchuk*

INSTRUCTIONS FOR USE

I have always loathed to read directions; I get anxious about sequentiality and the tiny print. Who follows directions to the letter anyway? I'll tell you who: the owners of things. Fluent readers and affluent people. Please feel at liberty to read this aloud to your pet or a ghost; read it out of order or homophonically; leave it on read or unread. This index is a memoir of dyslexia, which distills, palimpsests, or perhaps kills the real and unreadable primary text. What's re(a)d pools and beams here. This index leaks and stains your hands as you hold it in mind; it stutters, sounds out, and struggles to be digestible; it backtracks and questions itself as it attempts to organize illegibility. The text hopes you will join it in these acts of vocal color. Because color is indexical, both linguistically and visually, it is a primal way of shaping vision. Look for holes you can dive into; look for images you can swallow; move your eyes backwards or in concentric circles as you resist the text's chronology and linear logics; believe in its undulations; misread and daydream your way through. Might you read this sentence or just as well Johnnie Walker Red it?

Maraschino Cherry

The artificial preservation of a color in language. When my family moves near a park with cherry trees, I spend whole weekends climbing them; my daybreak fills with little birds and the spaces between leaves where the sky breaks through. I invite my own reasons to be there: the antelope, frog, rabbit, whale shapes the sky takes between branches. There, I can breathe. I spot my first real cherry and don't hesitate to devour it. These between-spaces held meaning, which hold me there. On the page, however, negative space is what must be ignored in order to read. Sometimes I'll do anything not to face a full page of text. Not to see, instead of words, eyes on the page—the animals staring back at me. Not to see the white rivers and black outlines of ghosts in the trees. Look over the contents, the notes, the index, the blurbs, the bio—stare at the author's photograph. Ask it, please, to read to me.

Alizarin Crimson

The dark, transparent trance of trying to read. At the kitchen table, my grandmother holds a flashcard. Its red word blares at me, holds me to it, my mind stuck and burning. While my mother's in the hospital and my dad is overseas, I am hers and not hers. A retired school teacher from Southern gentry, she waits for her triumph, but I am where things go awry. "Um," I say drawing out the vowel as if searching for a sound to bite off and fill my mouth like blood. What my grandmother wanted to remember and what she wanted to forget shuttle back and forth in a sanguinary churn. Blood is a motherfucking genius—it's the body's social organizer and memory tank. It remembers the tides and its plasma maintains the sea's deep recipe for ions. Yet it is poised to clot, to become solid if need be. We stare at each other. Her hand holding the card begins to shake slightly. "I don't know," I say, "alizarin crimson." She keeps her eyes fixed on mine, clenching her jaw. Then she says as if finishing a thought: "YET."

Cadmium

The color I imagine my living human insides to be—warm, muscular, toxic. Reading seems like a magic trick staged for others, or an act of divination, a holographic illusion. My body turns inside-out when I try it: heat on my neck and cheeks, sweat-skin, red stammer in my throat. My blushing pushes light years between me and the page; my viscera becomes the magnetized pole of yes-no. I get by on hunches and luck, figuring and refiguring. I assume postures of reading as if it were a kinetic activity. I pretend I can see through objects, see past the surface of things and into the future. Sure, I can imagine my own my gruesome death. I'm dead here on the page, where I rely on you in another time zone to bring me to life. You and a circle of bystanders begin to form like skin around my body, flayed on the pavement, guts spilling out, luminous viscera spelling out the next omen. When hidden reds are brought into the open—like ax oxide mineral extracted from a mine, like an ancient red ochre fresco found buried under a church floor—their color immediately dissolves into the blank light of day, already forgotten.

Amaryllis Red

An unfolding that demonstrates knowledge is always incomplete. I hold it in my hands like a book and focus inside the red frame. I turn the white plastic knobs, watching the point depart. To make lines on an Etch-a-Sketch is to not break the skin of myself. I audition a grey, gritty landscape. Tracks at dusk. All winter the same horizon. Then comes the lineography of an early amaryllis. Look hard, turn the flower into a face and back into an aurora borealis then a redwood. Consciousness flows round the rim, thinks with blood. Shake out a river and a hogback. A branch snaps. Is that my reflection looking back? Turn a mirror into a map, mountainscape, textscape. What does it say? Making a mark means scratching though the surface. Your line merely exposes the darkness already inside the toy. Whatever I draw withdraws into an abyss. What does it say? I trace the frame again and again, boxes inside boxes, thinking I am drawing something real, making a real thing. Reading wraps itself around the picture, a corruption of subject and object.

Rose

As a noun, an icon of love; as a verb, what you do in spite of having crashed. The first poem in my first book, which was also my dissertation, describes seeing a helicopter wrecked on a hill as a windmill then spins out into a catalogue of analogues--or, in hindsight, a catalogue of desperate misreadings. The poem ends here, with the narrator "giving her gift to the good world." At the time of publication, I was still closeted as a dyslexic, but that didn't stop me from making very little distinction between the textual and nontexual world. Where others see print, I see scenes and tableaux. W.G. Sebald's *Austerlitz* begins when the narrator discovers he can no longer read the phone book. He is like "a man who has been abroad a long time and cannot find his way through the urban sprawls anymore." A city of words becomes engulfed in an impenetrable fog. To what extent does reading take place within a reader's consciousness or out there, in a system separate from you or me? Letters become images of the very contingency of imaginative vision: operations of what can and cannot be seen, what is given and what is lost.

Burnt Sienna

When we can't see the red for the redness, the color for the place, the crayon name for fantasies of the namer. My card opens the wrong way. Loopy flowers spill over the card's face where I have scrawled "haqqy dirthbay!!" inside a heart. Do I imagine a dirthbay is the Bay of Dearth? Is it something to exclaim? The card is for my mother, but I have felt the Bay of Dearth as my own mythical birthplace, a watery lack lapping on the barren rocky shores, the outlines of which change so quickly that descriptions are futile. It is a place where anything is possible because everything is potential, like a page you stare into that does not give up its language but reveals itself in fathoms.

Permanent Magenta

The color of light seen through eyelids. You have watched people read. You assume you can do this, too; you are able to do many things easily, and this looks easy. You recognize a word here or there, a syllable. It says "rasp," "rest," or "test"—look at what it could be—"real," or "re-do." Is that what it means? A word could do so much for you if it just would. You hear a stutter in your head, you hear a voice spitting a sound. When "red" is "read," your vision is all body, not retinal. A word keeps swallowing me whole. Sentences swallow me, hold me under long suffocating paragraphs as if I were buried alive. Where did my anxiety end and dyslexia begin? "If Red is in everything," says Gertrude Stein, "it is not necessary."

Candy Apple

A round stain and a taste that changes the shape of your mouth. I curl up on our striped couch and hold a book in my lap. Reading was such a respected activity in my house, I could be sure no one would bother me. No one would order me outside or into chores; I could just hemorrhage time in peace. I let my mind stretch into its own far-fetched treetops and swirl into interstellar eons. I did not make up stories because I could not imagine resolutions. I could not link cause and effect or create ligatures between flashes. I wandered into mundane and absurd moments. I knew how to free associate and dissociate with equal ease. If I could make a grown man groan, I could read a few sentences, surely. I did not think about my grandfather's hands down my pants, or up my shirt, his face on my neck, his weight on top of me at night while my grandmother labored daily to teach me to read. That part was easy to leave out. There were no words for it. Those afternoons I was abandoned by text, I was not on his lap then. And this story, if you can call it that, does not end that way.

Paprika

A semblance of truth. Having fond memories of being buoyed by its wholesome story, my mother urges the *Little House on the Prairie* series on me. Every night I take the books to bed where I pretend to read them. Not pretend exactly, more like simulate. As if reading were merely a physical sport, I run my eyes over the words in preparation for their holographic revelations. I may as well be looking for a station on a short-wave radio. There's nothing but static until suddenly I latch onto a recognizable phrase and plunge face first into a vivid experience. I hear the words, their sounds destroying vertigo, offering me solid ground. Every book is an audio book; even when no one is reading aloud, I hear it. I hear Ma, Pa, Laura and Mary on the windy Prairie, I see them gathered around the hearth. I stay with them until the internal rhythm of my own voice's silent reading leads me back to my own thinking. I slip back into daydreams, white noise filling the page once again. I read entire novels as a sequence of discrete vignettes or poems, moments of sensation and narration rubbing together, erasing connection.

Geranium Lake

The red you sleep through, the red that only exists in dreams. If red were to fall asleep, it would mock human dishonesty. It would use up time and dream of its opposite. Red runs ahead and cannot wait for me. My body is a dream that mocks its own imagination. Reading is a dream of my body flying. My body is a dream that produces red by itself. Sentences streak by: book, book, book, pen. Vivid swaths of red ink on the page, so vibrant it seems to hum just above its own stain. If red were to wake after two hundred years, it would find itself the object of *Tender Buttons*. Red doesn't bifurcate into subject and object; no: the word runs where the world runs out: "Out of kindness comes redness and out of rudeness comes rapid same question." To put reading in the past tense means to turn the page red.

Hematite

Nostalgia for a missing memory that colors all remembrance. Unlike most writers, I have no childhood memories of being lazily absorbed in a book, turning pages in the car, at the beach, out back, or in my room while the darkness gathered gently around me. I have no nostalgia for a favorite book and a favorite chair at the public library where I might find the person I waited to become: teenager, glamorous, beloved, Olympian, living my own life. Remember, the child Jane Eyre reading her book of birds behind folds of scarlet drapery? Her reading is shot through with fog and rainclouds, and her adamant sense of elsewhere. If I could have abandoned my own suffocating house, escaped or reclaimed myself this way, believe me, I would have. Instead, not-reading sharpened my mental flights. Not-reading, I listened out and in, a voltage alternating through me. Not-reading enlarged and multiplied my senses, then contracted them powerfully. I don't whine and cry when I don't get what I want, I know how to steal.

Oxblood

A red that runs, like a finger along the edge of a flame, or a noise that escapes your own mouth. When words run out into time, they create their own suspense. Every sentence is a plot. I hang on, one word at a time. When I hear a word, it is already disappearing. Literacy overhauls our temporal sense. Time to a literate person is a passage; time flows, it flies and unfolds like a river or a road. We mark time with words. To a literate person, time heals. Literacy creates a line of thinking, it strings you along with links of causality. It reasons and pretends there is always a reason. When you read, you see a phrase fixed in space, arrested in time, escaped into landscape. You create fictional time as you murder real time. You read to sense a doubling of time—then you slip entirely out of sync. Unlike being in a place, being in a text means keeping ourselves separate, distinct from the page, looking at it from a distance, where we can't help but consider it analytically, aesthetically. Yet when I read, I hear what I'm reading as if it were coming from inside me. I hear it in several diegetic and mimetic ways—expressed as sensual immersion in characters as well as narratorial voices, as an internal commentary responding to the text, and as a vocal imaginary that could never foist itself into "real" time—that run, blurring into one sound containing the buzz of everything around it.

Maroon

Not being able to tell the difference between being lost and being dumb. My mother often fell into voices, accents, and intentional mispronunciations. She might, imitating Bugs Bunny, look out the window and flamboyantly call our neighbor a "maroon," instead of using the word "moron." The word "moron," itself coined by a psychologist in the early 1900s, performs its own meaning when misread or mispronounced. How dumb can you get? To equate "moron" with "maroon" though implies a sonic relationship between abandonment and idiocy. To be illiterate is to feel marooned, isolated, left. It took humans two thousand years to develop literacy, and now we give a new human about two thousand days until we expect her to start reading. It takes nurturing and practice. I might have been taken for an idiot, but very few adults even noticed I couldn't read. Or maybe they abandoned me upon noticing. I made my way on my wits and changing schools. It's an urban myth that prison officials use third grade reading scores to predict the number of future beds they'll need. But it's not a myth that kids who can't read well in third grade are four times less likely to graduate high school; add poverty and racism to this equation and the number triples. Kids who don't graduate high school are twenty-three times more likely to end up in jail.[1] If you consider the other meaning of Maroon—an escaped slave living in the Caribbean—you see how abandoment is just what you choose to ignore, an oxymoron.

Red Cross Red

The red lithium turns when ground into powder, bursting in fireworks. My mother liked to read to calm and escape herself. When I was a girl I savored her gentle, gravel voice reading stories aloud to me, punctuated by drags on her cigarette. One day when I'm home sick from school, she reads me a biography of Clara Barton. She does it, though she says I'm too old to be read to, acknowledging both its pleasures and efficacy, how much better I seem to absorb information when listening. I don't say: that's because I can't read. I want to stay in her bed, steady among the vast blankets and her smoker's voice transporting me to another time. Clara Barton was a nurse, like both of my aunts, and I could easily imagine her story becoming mine. Yet the book my mother reads me says nothing of Barton's involvement in suffrage and civil rights movements, or her fight for equal pay for women and her refusal to marry. The best part of Barton's story—her resistance—was entirely left out in favor of her capacity to comfort sick and injured men. My mother did not note these absences; she may have even created them, erasing and rewriting the narrative as she read. She was skilled at refusing to acknowledge what she didn't like. In other words, this story was her kind of fiction, if not her kind of life.

Allura Red

To make naturally red things redder by neurochemistry. The brain is not naturally wired to read. Unlike speech, we must build new neural pathways in order to do it. As you learn the skill of reading, you create and reinforce these connections. Slowly, imprecisely, inflexibly, we change our brains to become literate. Literacy then shapes how we comprehend and how we think, which we integrate biologically and culturally, each act coloring the other. Picture the back of someone walking away, alone, with a book to find a quiet place to read. With this, a reader develops a complex conception of personal identity. We isolate ourselves and surround ourselves with abstractions. Silent reading is a place of suspension, reservation, exception, identified with the Protestant spirit of skeptical thinking for oneself. Now picture this reader walking back to us, walking back to sociality and interactivity. Excited by the book, she is eager to discuss it, testing and honing ideas about what she has read. These two distinct movements have become naturalized as a basic intellectual process.

Brick

The walls of schools in small towns, from the Latin root "to break." Simon Weil says it's impossible to look at a text and not read it; her account of the automaticity and immediacy of reading—which she says, is as natural as feeling the cool wet current of your hand in running water, letting it wash over you transparently, as it delivers its sudden, full sensation— astonishes me. If that's how it is, if *seeing* text means *reading* it; if meaning and sensation hit without involving the text's materialities, then what I'm doing must be something else. In Colorado then Pennsylvania, as the new girl in two different middle schools, I would sit, quiet and nervous, at my table during our government-mandated 15 minutes of Silent Sustained Reading [SSR] until either time was up, or the huge effort I exerted on the page made it break into sound, a visceral audition, by force of will, came gushing out so loudly, the book seemed to be shouting at me. I could not turn the volume down. The book's aural qualities and physical objectness swell together in the word "volume." Out of a volumizing consciousness, out of shifting voices, out of a choral tuning, comes a stunned consciousness that hears reading out loud, one word at a time.

Quinacridone Red

Reminds us that anything may turn red. Certain foxes, pandas, squirrels, and jellyfish; male cardinals; cooked lobsters; the neck of the largest wallaby; the nose of a mandrake or alcoholic; a mandrill's ass; the second horse of the Apocalypse. Text writhes and breathes, it undulates and swims, it hides, but will not turn red for me. My face turns, words dying in my mouth. Words like animals dying sad deaths. When I read the Red List, I'm not only reading an elegy for endangered species. It is a catalogue of vulnerability that stands for an epic. What doesn't get classified— whatever's rendered economically, aesthetically, or culturally worthless— becomes invisible, unreadable.

Red List Red

The viscera that leaks out of an elegy. Blood presses to my skin as if it were a window, it stirs and waits. My father wants to know why I'm wearing a hat in the middle of summer. His question accuses, "Aren't you hot?" I tell him, "that's not a hat, that's my face." You see a red hat on the first coin in America. It was the cap of *liberté, élgalité,* and *fraternité* during the French Revolution, and since Roman times, the sign of the manumitted slave. Michael Brown wore a red cap the day a cop shot him. I do not wear a red hat, but I understand why my father sees one on me. My blush is a mask inside a fantasy. When I think of my father's question, I think of his eyes on me, disgusted. I think several things at once and the impossibility of expressing them simultaneously is where *eros* begins. I make sense of my feeling by remembering being looked at while reading aloud—overwhelmed, paralyzed, vulnerable to the looker, whose eyes pursue me both as prey and as conquest.

Blush

A sign of ripeness, a full sugary expression of vitality and vanity. Darwin offers an effusive explanation, performing the sputtering, exposed, declarative feeling of blushing in his notebooks:

> Blush is intimately concerned with thinking of ones [sic] appearance—does the thought drive blood to surface exposed, face of man, face, neck, upper/bosom in women: like erection | shyness is certainly very much connected with thinking of oneself.--\blushing\ is connected with the sexual, because each sex thinks of what another thinks of him, than of any one of his own sex --. Hence, animals, not being such thinking people, do not blush.—sensitive people [are] apt to blush.

Red Round Globe Hot Burning[2]

Shot with a tranquilizer dart, this red woke up startled and somewhere else. We were going around the room taking turns reading from our Sex Education textbook in the sixth grade. I counted paragraphs and students between me and the current reader, so that I could silently practice my part. I knew the consequences of not being prepared. Everyone's attention on me amplified my dysfluency, and no one dropped an eye from my boiling face. Red is the color of being looked at, and I was my own vivid illumination. Even waiting, in anticipation, I lit up. Someone went to the bathroom and my turn would have to be the long paragraph on ejaculation, which I had not practiced. There are moments we are unprepared for and are better for it, but this time, I was fucked. I was a thing rising in the lap of a boy who inexplicably cannot come to the front of the room to put his answer on the board. Then I began the onerous task of keeping my eyes ahead of my voice. I felt only the red alert of my blood pounding. I tried to say the words as if there were mine, but I fumble them. I stutter, correct, fixate on the wrong word then backtrack. I am not making sense; I am feeling words like eyes all over my skin, blinking. I jump ahead then down, nervously spewing uncontrolled sounds, an awful, unwanted ejaculation.

Day-Glo Red

A color as relentless as reading itself, it keeps coming without rest. How I know that reading is artificial to the human brain, is that I quickly forget what I read. It takes an effort to retain after the effort of performance; I look at the red sky for a few minutes until it fades and then turns dark. But now I remember: I did have a favorite book as a child, *The Guinness Book of World Records*. It's the illiterate's bible, or was in the 1970s. Looking at pictures, looking at bodies, imagining a future for my body, in these pages I aspired toward flaunting difference in black and white like the fat twins on motorcycles with matching tiny white cowboy hats; the man from India with the longest fingernails, curled like a plant; the tallest man standing beside the shortest; the woman with the smallest waist looking like she can't breathe; the determined look on the face of the longest long jumper, flying feet first. But I did not want to be the person who keeps reading the same sentence over and over for days on end or the girl whose fierce blush outlasts everyone's.

Estrus red

Red punctuation in the field of red things. Sometimes at twelve years old, I feel invisible, like a ghost haunting my own life. The marks I can't read are proof that I don't exist. I get out of bed to prove I'm real enough, can't sleep. It's dark but on the floor, I see three drops of blood that fell after a poison apple lodges in Snow White's throat. I stoop down to wipe the blood drops. Another drop. I don't know yet where I'm bleeding. Drop, drop. Panic ripples across the room. I wipe up the blood drops, but the rims remain. They cling to the floor in O-shapes, a trail of stains mouthing my own astonishment back to me. These open mouths will not reply, not in a thousand years or a pure instant. Yet what in the dark doesn't know the danger of leaving no trace? What in the text doesn't know the danger of leaving no trail?

Infra-Red

Red cellophane over a flashlight will help you read a map at night. A safelight lets you see the photograph as it begins to appear in the darkroom. After watching the black and white eyes take shape, I can no longer look back in color. Developing in a room so dark that no walls were visible, my body's depths broke through my face. Even thinking about being called on to read aloud, I flamed out. I sometimes pretended not to know where we were in the text—something I learned from kids who probably were bored or truly spacing out—in hopes for a verbal reprimand and ultimately to be skipped over. How could I say out loud what I heard in my head as I read? I'm surprised how easily I split it two: I read, I think; the text and the mind feed one another. Reading's capacity to illicit thinking held me captive, but I could not perform it for a class even if my teacher asked me to, which she didn't. I could push off from the text, go beyond what was written into my own ideas, transformations, questions, and speculations; I could not simply read what was there.

Bullseye Red

The ability to make anything a target, the red eyes of a photograph of me when I wasn't looking. At least not looking at you. In the photo, I am digging clay out of a stream, my jeans rolled up so that my knees peer out like eyes full of emptiness. Coral snake eyes, mole rat eyes, the eyes of crows during copulation, millions of worm eyes. To see through language as we see through color: not the words but the red eyes, the compound eyes reading each sentence simultaneously in six different ways. In a letter, Emily Dickinson describes her eyes, "like the Sherry in the Glass, that the Guest leaves." But it is difficult to see with red eyes; rather, it is difficult to be certain that red isn't appropriating everything it draws near. The tiny scarlet eyes of cicadas dig themselves out of the earth every seventeen years. My eyes digging out of a sentence, a red tide irrupts between the eye and what the eye wants.

Pantone Red

When colors do not actually exist except in language, how do you match them? When one day I call my shirt "dusty rose," my older brother insists it's "rooster-red." I chalk it up to a version of male colorblindness until adults take his side. Even then, it took a paint swatch to convince me. My brother's favorite color had always been blue, pitting his will against mine. How could it be that I failed to perceive the color I love best in the world? What is the corrective to see what I want and adore? What is the treatment to see only what's there? What greater human affliction: our blindness toward affinity and love.

Blood stripe

A certain red streak drawn up from the depths of militant minds. Every three weeks, we found our new seats by looking for our tests laid out on desks from top to lowest scores. My high school algebra teacher, a discharged Marine who committed suicide two years after I graduated, expected me to be as brilliant a student as my brother had been the year before. He did not appreciate being wrong about me, and he did not appreciate being asked why or what for, questions that hoped for context and motivation. This time, I didn't get the goat seat, but I never made it past the middle of the room. When he asked me to write a problem out on the board, I chalked slowly, checking and rechecking my numbers, making sure I did not write 21 as 12. My focus breaks, however as he grabs my bra strap through my shirt, pulls and lets go, as if it were a sling shot. It happens faster than it takes to read this sentence. I freeze. I hear students around me giggle. There was no way to know what he meant to communicate. Had I done the problem incorrectly? It was not the first time he had snapped my bra, but it was the first time I had not laughed along with my classmates. I knew even then that this harassment is what I got for not being an "A" student.

Cardinal

A flutter in your stomach and in the greenest trees; multiple speeds of being that catch on each other and pull holes in time where whole lives fall through. Pity the text that relies on me to perform it. I spew a palimpsest of guesses. My voice harbors remnants of disarticulation and consolidates the anxiety of writing itself. Can you hear my vocal stumbling as a gesture toward linguistic complexity? My voice involuntarily indexes the time of thinking and the time of reading, the time of experience and the time of vocalization, the time of causation and the time of digression, the time of blitzkrieging through a chaos of phonemes and the time of processing my own panic, the time of contented absorption and the time of agitated humiliation. Paradox shudders between temporal realms. Confected time lags behind annexed time, an emergency of minutes mismatches the daydreamt surplus of seconds, the book's time graphed over my own. Asynchronous perceptions of time create an inner out-of-sync feeling. My thoughts speed ahead and sideways, every which-way, as the slow steady decoding keeps another beat. I tap my foot to keep the text in rhythm. My mind flies off and the text plods onward. Time stops moving as I move through it.

Ruddy or Ruby

Unacknowledged and acknowledged reds colliding: the dangers of misreading, the delights. In the 18th and 19th centuries, when greater access to texts and education created conditions for mass literacy in Europe, explicit concerns about reading proliferated. Reading a novel might freak you out, change your mind, make you cry or seize the entire day. Many saw reading as a special threat to children and discouraged it with a swift kick out of doors. The sight of a child reading the morning away alarmed the pedagogues who warned: "compulsive reading is a foolish and harmful abuse of an otherwise good thing, truly a great evil, as contagious as the yellow fever in Philadelphia."[3] The implication is not simply that obsessive or unsupervised reading is damaging but that the example of doing it—reading in public—will lead others to want to try it for themselves. Reading is contagious and addictive. And eventually I learn to savor its difficulty, the capacity to read slowly, to practice contemplative reading, through poetry. In college, once I discovered poetry, the reading field leveled. Slow reading became a virtue, like the capacity to close read a poem, first as a stay against the allure of "speed reading," then as a stay against screen skimming and the accumulations of capitalist consumerism. Poetry's phenomenology, the way that it treats perception, tells the story of reading that's dense and deliberate, that's quirky, private, creative, playful, willful, materially driven, and temporally plural, the kind of reading I have always practiced. To read poetry well is to hear it because it teaches readers to listen sensually and analytically, semantically and structurally. Poetry makes use of differing somatic rhythms; it doesn't ask you to deny them. Poetry folds into itself the problem of reading, and each poem offers its own hermeneutics. To read poetry is to put yourself in the subject position of a dyslexic.

"Sunburnt Mirth!"

Copying out John Keats' poems as a kinetic attempt to have written them, lacking both an object and language and yet needing a future.[4] To John Keats, a reader is someone who voyages through the black and white labyrinths of text, following uncertain routes into expansive fields, trompe-l'oeil hills, trap doors, staircases, and sunsets. "What delicious diligent indolence" he called reading—a robust, serious meandering that provokes and accumulates inner resonances and associations. Is it possible to read "blushful" in Keats's "Ode to a Nightingale" without also reading "bushful" or "blissful?" My reading comes slowly, like a blush, with great vulnerably; it is my secret sun, a burning mirth.

Carmine

The color of your face as you watch yourself cry in the mirror hoping to recognize in it the source of your pain. I take an Intro to Psychology class in college, reveling in each new set of symptoms. I believe I've lived or loved all the conditions I read about, until a forlorn note of pure recognition hits under the subheading "dyslexia." On the phone with my mother later I say, I think I have it. Oh yes, she replies, you were diagnosed with that in kindergarten. I sit down on the floor. What? I pull out bits of lint and dirt in the carpet. We thought you'd grow out of it, she offers blithely. This is how I learned to cover up my shame, as my mother had, by pretending it was something I might outgrow like baby teeth or pigtails. No one had inquired further or bothered to let me know. I bulldozed my way down the page, clumsy and determined, year after year until I believed in my own work ethic. Until the very source of my pride derived from a dyslexia-made-determination and refusal to be left behind. I accepted my mother's story once again. I had already learned to compensate, to fake and hide. I'm not now going to turn back into someone who can't read.

Rusty

A weakness hidden by neglect. I don't want the cage the diagnosis "dyslexia" puts around me; I don't want your pity or suspicion. Why does the label both feel like a confirmation and an outrage, a relief and a lie? I don't want it or use it. My feelings obstruct each other and hold me in a kind of deadlock. I'm sure I don't belong in the ranks of English majors, or would-be-writers, or even college-goers, and I don't want anyone finding out my fraud. I will go on as I have always been, a scofflaw. I go incognito, and the days get on. I go into them as someone raised to dress the part, putting on my school clothes and playing The Reader. In this way I was saved from the machinery of "achievement," but not from its engine, disappointment. There seemed no way to imagine myself without a costume. I will go on impersonating a reader the way I impersonated "female" as a teenager, the way I posed as "smart" even as I puked red wine out of a moving window, the wild cabaret ribbon flying from my mouth into open air. Some things cannot be fully swallowed: "Maybe happiness is like the foam of the painful tide of life that covers our souls with red fullness."[5]

Vermilion

A red that metastasizes inside the mind. Reading is alchemic, created by operations of extraction, distillation and transformation. I run my eyes over lines of words to hypnotize myself. Instead of giving myself mystically to the author's world, I leap from one word to the next as if words are stepping stones to my own mind, and sentences were runways inward. The physical sensation of saccade and drift rhythmizes my thinking. In class, I deliver a long, nervous disposition on why the word "mediate" is the key to the poem we are studying. I say it's talismanic, I say the whole poem hinges on this word. Having a moment of synaptic insight, I thought the room was riveted. When someone quietly pointed out the word was "meditate," I realized their silence was a polite cringe. "Mediate" is probably a back formation of the word "meditate," to measure, to think, but that comes later and consoles little. Poetry links these words, the bodily rhythms of meditation and the social rhythms of mediation. I don't remember anything else about the poem now.

Carnelian

A process for experiencing time. The rooms in the dorm all contained the same four pieces of furniture mirrored on each side. I moved from desk to bed to chair to table and back again. I hung a secret mirror on the back of the door, where I could see the whole room reflected: I became a force of flatness, a *Girl Reading* (Picasso), assuming the shapes of furniture; I became *Young Woman Reading* (Cassatt), I became *Woman Reading* (Matisse) or *Young Girl Reading* (Fragonard) or *Girl Reading a Letter at an Open Window* (Vermeer). The effortless softness of those paintings made reading seem like sleeping, their red light, red cushions, red dresses, and their strands of red-hair coming lose. A book lends a girl the feeling of being lost so that you can save her. All of the girls and women labor together, silently sounding out the words. Many details go unrecorded. My eyes slip off the line, down the page. I saw my body in the painting, in the mirror, in the film, in the Instagram post, in the dream sucked back into another life or propelled forward so far out of mine, I was transported into my own desire. My mind slides; my face in the mirror says the words aloud in order to keep myself here, in order to exist beyond the plane of the book. A teacher once told me that he could read me like a book. I lived as if "well-read" meant "ready." I confused text's elusiveness with eroticism. The blush of shame tangled with a sexual flush. I put the book down, electrified and exhausted by chasing language through my body, pursing it, longing for it. Inevitably language pools in my cunt where, I can to take it from there.

Auburn

A stain that cannot be removed or hidden with a rug. My professor's entire apartment was red—carpets, curtains, furniture, the kitchen cabinets were lined with hot sauces. Entering it took some breath. Her glassy-eyed dog greeted me with abandon, leaping around me like a flame. That sunless winter, while dog-sitting for her, an electromagnetic field of vermilions buffered me from the city. I was inside a fire that needed no stoking, a fire that smelled like flora, where eyes seemed to be hiding. I dyed my hair vivid auburn making a stain on her bathroom floor for which she later scolded me. My boyfriend could not stand to come over; he said he felt swallowed. He said he is not a boner machine. I slipped into one of her red robes and read my own sentences. Red erases "read," and reverses the vertigo of habit. Rimbaud says "I" is red, "smile of beautiful lips / in anger or in the raptures or penitence." True, "I" is a mixed bag of ambivalences, as attracted to linguistic confusion as "red" itself: a somber red ocher from Sinope on the Black Sea begat the medieval color *sinople*, which could be either red or green. On a shelf in her apartment, I discover she has written a book called *Mood Swings*. Living two months in that red apartment, though I felt simpler, I became saturated and ascendant. My body seemed stretched, gravity-resistant, like a figure in a mannerist painting and making the most of it. Or like one of those tiny female figures engulfed in Matisse's magisterial *Red Studio* (1911). Matisse says "A certain red has an effect on your blood pressure," and more: a fleet of reds speeds your lungs, stings your nose, it hollows bones. I walked her blind dog three times around the block three times a day; I sat in the red rooms and rarely left. When I did, green followed me, burst forth from a secret germination. Grassy snowbanks piled around verdant buildings, as I walked through the mesmerizing green stream of faces. After my excursion, I unlocked the little red door to my temporary Mars. Here was my booster shot, far exceeding the basic daily requirement. I became a chronic user of red.

Scarlet

A shade of redundancy. I do not have my childhood Little Red Riding Hood costume in mind when I dress up for a Halloween party. Nonetheless, I wear red from wig to cowboy boots—glue on some plastic flies and call myself a scab or an open wound depending on who I'm talking to. Maybe I dress this way to disguise my red face. Red moves deep down in the red; not easy to read, though my dress means to undress in the least sexy way. Can you separate the costume from the face it extends? "The surfaces of clothing are facial," says Alphonso Lingis, the philosophy professor whose house is the scene of the party. I entered the party through his front door, which juts out between two wide windows of a sleeping porch filled with huge white cockatoos. To enter into the nose of a house is to become a smell. *Had you hoped to smell like roses?* The question hawked up like blood, the taste of which makes me salivate. To smell blood is to know vulnerability and decide which side of it you are on.

Herring Red

The menstrual stain in underwear. I quietly get dressed and leave early, before he wakes. Walking home, I try to pocket my hands, but they shoot right through to my thighs. As we slept, his dogs ate out both pockets of my leather jacket. Before that, he had pulled out my tampon and threw it to those two big dogs, as if it were a red rubber ball. Years later, I read another writer's account of this same moment, her own small shock of amusement and horror as she watches the bloody tampon fly then land as a bone or stick the dogs fight over. I think about writers' rituals and rehearsals before or during writing. I'm disorientated, sleepy, happy, and disappointed at the predictability of my attractions—as if fucking writers might bring me closer to language. As if sleeping with them meant sleeping with their sentences, their enjambments, their plot swerves. A train going by prolongs my confusion. I don't have any tampons. I'm trying to make it home before the blood soaks through my pants. But this is a red herring, a visual distraction that I pretend is the reason for my hurry away.

Mahogany

In sunlight, prone to turning the darkest dark. Reading aloud to my daughter, I feel her judgement. Or worse, I feel her normalizing each mistake and backtrack, each sentence I begin again. I want to shelter her from the contamination of my voice. I want you to catch my drift instead. Are you at least misreading some of what I write here? Can you wolf it down in whole paragraphs? Does my drive to reproduce an exact replica of my thinking in your mind feel dangerous? As you read, can you hear my voice in your head? Does this sentence reach for your hand across the table? My difficulty reading writes large the materiality of language and its processes, its recursivity and accumulations, its sonic and visual properties. Text that refuses to acknowledge the provisional nature of thought spooks me. I bring my own instability to it. I have to pay attention, to use each word's complete self, to roll each one on my tongue, to map it on the page, to vibrate with it in the air ringing.

Dragon's Blood

The violent absence of color in a blank mirror.

Dear Dr. Hume: The HIV/AIDS Notification Service is a voluntary organization based at the Mount Sinai Hospital in New York City, which works with people who have recently tested positive for the Human Immune Deficiency Virus (HIV). One of our purposes is to provide confidential health care information. The other is to notify those who have been sexually active with someone who has recently tested positive for HIV. Your name was submitted to our organization, for possible contraction of HIV. Someone you have sexual contact with, has tested positive for the Human Immune Deficiency Virus, and has requested our services as a means of anonymously informing all past and present sexual partners of their possible contraction.

This is a notification of complete anonymity. Therefore, we are unable to provide you with the name of the person who has contracted HIV and submitted your name to us. We recommend that you be tested as soon as possible, as early detection is one of the best defenses. Because of the serious nature of this life-threatening illness, we want to make sure all relevant parties, including your husband are informed. We are truly sorry for what you and your family are now facing, but take hope in the fact that people are now living longer, healthier, normal lives, in spite of being HIV positive.

Sincerely,
The Volunteers of the HIV/AIDS Notification Service

"Livid Final Flame"[6]

The burning that dwells in the brain, colors perception. The words drop so fast I can't pick them up. Tips of matches with their quick gigantic life. Reading this letter is a struggle; I re-read it many times as comprehension slowly blooms. Later, reading it aloud on the phone to ex-lovers rehearses the struggle. Anxiety injects itself into the act of reading—heart racing, eyes frantically skipping ahead and coiling back, illegibility compounded with emotional refusal, a million questions flooding the page. I want at that moment to not know how to read, to unknown what I've read, to forget my hard-won literacy. Reading the letter feels endlessly recursive and transports me to an earlier time when reading itself was the subject of everything I read.

Inflamed

Red that burns beyond extinguishing, beyond extinction. Simone Weil writes:

> Everyone has felt the effect of bad news that one reads
> in a letter or newspaper: one feels oneself seized, bowled
> over, as if by a blow, before having understood what is
> the matter; and long afterward [at] the mere sight of the
> letter… a more vivid pain wells up, itself, sudden and
> piercing like a physical pain, seizing as if it came from
> outside—as if it dwelt in this piece of paper the way the
> burning dwells in a fire.

Madder

A latent synesthesia waking up inside you as you pass through the words, entering the whole feeling. Read this as if you are part of an infinite universe, not able to stand safely outside it where I can't touch you. Like John Keats, I want you, dear reader, with me, passing into my lines, dragging baggage through "the coming musk-rose, full of dewy wine / The murmurous haunt of flies on summer eves." This redness talks to my wounds, it corresponds. Each phrase triggers a liquid imagination that gives pulse. This is the fundamental sense of Keats's insistence on "Negative Capability": a constant unsettling of the poetic, forcing each trajectory of thought to walk the plank, again and again, to a provisional end where it must hang for a moment on the brink of its own extinction, until the reader, in an imaginative leap, fills in the blank, creates and recreates meaning. I don't, after all, have HIV or AIDS, but I know that reading is an unanswerable question I ask and ask with my body.

Rash Red

An itch that can't be reached on sleepless nights. My daughter's tutor tells me that because my dyslexia went untreated, I probably never forged the neural bridges necessary to read in the most efficient way. I'm probably still reading like a first grader, but one with over forty years' experience. I recall a friend, in his first years on the job as a poetry professor, laughing about a young woman in his graduate class who, he says, mistakes her disability for talent. She is a pitiful faker who vamps up her language deficits and regards her dyslexic tendencies as poetic techniques. I feel shame for her, caught in all the shame I have held back and all the shame I imagine she is not feeling. I missed out on remaking my brain into something more contemporary. I didn't exactly flaunt my difference, but by stranding myself in my incompetencies, I secretly strengthened my blind spots. The instability of my reading offered possibilities for pluralistic insights and less habitual or brutal meanings. Skipping the practical skill and speeding right to the conceptual delights of reading, I not only gained an ability to imagine, I lost knowledge about the world, about real things, in equal measure. I come with a humiliated relation to literacy; I understood early how language, as a system of displacements and associations, is always screwing over someone. Yet as a writer and professor, I've devoted my life to reading. I was determined to discipline it, to counter-humiliate it: "It exhausts me to watch you / Flickering like that."[7]

"Little Bloody Skirts!"[8]

Red's revolutionary voice; a mouth, bloodied and still singing. I grow a third ear, another mouth. I become a third person while reading—not an author, not a reader, but a listener, negotiating all the readers and writers between us, all the voices marked by my stuttering gallops into mental sound storms, my missed takes: stab and guess, stab and guess. I'm producing the imaginary sound I'm hearing, prompted by the text and atopically dispersed in time. I'm reaching through the thin film of time in order to keep becoming: a reader becomes so through reading, as long as the text lasts. Anyone who has ever felt bereft upon finishing a book understands this transformation, which is both temporary and, in some measure, permanent: you can't go back, you have changed.

Sinopia

A pigment used for drafting frescoes; later used on Scantron tests. Is the shift away from print culture and reading inevitable? We fear a post-literate world, perhaps even a hyper-literate world, with cognitive attachments or extensions via technology (audiobooks), pharm (neuroenhancers), and biological developments (telepathy) that might be more powerful and faster than print. *The Literacy Foundation* illustrates this general anxiety about the end of reading in a series of promotional posters that depict critically ill fairy tale characters. In one, Cinderella is hooked up to an IV with the tagline, "When a child doesn't read, imagination disappears." The irony of this image is that the Brothers Grimm collected and modified traditional folk tales from a disappearing oral culture, writing them down, and locking them in to the now-familiar print versions. Read: video killed the radio star.

Cinnabar

A wavering iridescence between mythological colors and what's visible. When I visit my estranged father, who is dying of cancer, I try to set him up to deliver meaningful or at least kind affirmations, but I only set up myself. "I don't know," he replies, "we just thought we weren't as bright as your brother." To be red is to be infected—rubella, scarlet fever, greed, lust, debt, language, anger. Red-handed. To be caught red-eyed. Some women have eyes with two different red pigments, an extra cone uniquely enabling them to see whole enriched spectrums of red. They go around seeing things imperceptible to the fathers, who see through their fantasies.

Poppy

The hair of a witch; the ass of a spanked child. Only when red leaves the woods and moves into the mind does it become hot, florid, excessive, raw, siren-like. Even though I understand why, it embarrasses me—horrifies me—that I did not bother to investigate dyslexia until my own daughter was diagnosed over twenty years after my mother let the cat out of the bag. Even then, I kept my research focused on how I might help her. Any neurological understanding of dyslexia, any remediation techniques, any compensatory "gifts" associated with it, I laminate onto her. I had already been left to drift into delinquency: now what? I would not repeat the cycle. But what was I also teaching my daughter by not facing directly the ways in which this difference we shared had shaped my life?

Burgundy

The color of a mystery and the place it took hold. Cognitive linguists call the unconscious and automatic processes that account for fluent reading "systematicity." It's jerks of verse recited from furtive half glances, half-registered words we fill in or finish. Systematicity allows us to forget what we see when we read; the text dissolves so that we may hallucinate meaning and scene. What we see is what we release from the page. There's a certain amount of uncertainty in reading, of hypothesis, trance, and going on your nerve. Oliver Sacks describes a man who picks up a newspaper one morning but can't read it. He thinks he might be holding a Serbo-Croatian or Korean newspaper.[9] He is strangely calm, unfazed by this anomaly, perhaps because he doesn't remember the pleasures of reading, perhaps because he thinks his condition is temporary, or perhaps because it is a relief from the burden of reading. His vision otherwise seemed unimpaired. Eventually, doctors determine that the man woke up with alexia. Dyslexia often finds itself in the company of alexia, the sudden inability to read, and hyperlexia, the ability to read fluently without instruction usually by age three. Unlike alexia, with hyperlexia and dyslexia, you either are or aren't—there's no sudden onset or cure. The difference is that hyperlexia is often considered a super-ability, though it most often occurs with a complete lack of understanding the text. In other words, we value the performance of reading more than anything else about it.

Russet

A splendid chemical wedding of repulsion and revelation. I pause, reread a sentence in my student's final reflection paper: "I can't be bothered to read long passages of text." I find this sentence so stunningly offensive in the context of a Creative Writing class, with me as her only audience, that I have to examine my own reaction to it. My student's self-assured attempt to correct class requirements as she admits to not completing them baffles me. Her assertion comes as an affront to the very principles of the class, that reading and writing go hand in hand. No English teacher would likely find her statement palatable, but I'm also sure my own struggles to read inform my repulsion. Her caviler dismissal trivializes a major anxiety of my life and makes me doubt its inevitability. Would I have been better off not caring about reading? Might I have been someone who made a resource of her strengths, not her vulnerabilities and incapacities? Of course, this student's statement may in fact be a defense against her own difficulties reading. But then, anyone coming to writing with an absolute sense of their own linguistic competency isn't going to stick with it long enough to cultivate the skill. With that I know that there's no getting over it.

Paradoxical Red

A red that allows me to exist, but that only itself exists in language. John Keats assumes all readers have creative capabilities commensurate to writers and that all readers can be self-educating citizens. Keats robin-hoods the authority of the author in order to enable and truly employ the reader, and so equalize the relationship between reader and writer. He claims this horizontal relationship between readers and writers is analogous to a democratic relationship between citizens and elected officials; each must put forth equal amounts of effort in order to earn meaningful texts/contexts. Fernando Pessoa embodies a less utopian vision of the same process:

> I have never been able to read a single book to which I give myself over entirely; at each step, always, the incessant commentary of intelligence and imagination interrupted the thread of the narrative. After a few minutes, it was I who was writing the book—and what I wrote nowhere existed.

Propositional Red

A machine for momentarily capturing the gap between language use and perception.

Ludwig Wittgenstein: "To be able generally to name a color, is not the same as being able to copy it exactly. I can perhaps say 'There I see a reddish place' and yet I can't mix a color that I recognize as being exactly the same"

Rosmarie Waldrop: "I had inferred from pictures that the world was real…"

Ludwig Wittgenstein: "Is that connected with the fact that white gradually eliminates all contrasts, while red doesn't?"

Rosmarie Waldrop: "Though a speck in the visual field must have some color, it need not be red."

Brake-light Red

A red that thinks in blots and spasms. This is the essay of someone who doesn't know how to read or write, who almost doesn't know how to speak. Words flood my mouth like an onslaught, but they enter my eye slowly, stingily like wary strangers. I have no happier or more rational expectation of reading than I do of being dead, murdered by my lack of belonging in text. Yet being ravished by what I read is my first disability as a writer: less red is less of a sign, more of an outburst, a pinprick on a map becoming the capital. Red is the beginning of being, a red cell accumulating meaning, when an animal was a kind of plant, reactive and self-replicating, a contamination that is a poem or a root crushed into ancient dyestuffs. Its discursive yield is to disclose eidetic consciousness. Yet. Yet the sorrow of reading's tangled magnetism stops me in my tracks, spectralizes me. Yet I read to feel myself fully emerge in the red.

Endnotes

1 PolitiFact.com
2 Blake, William
3 Hoche, Gottfried (1762-1863) quoted in Arnim Polster
4 Robert Gluck delivered this story at Eastern Michigan University in March 2014, a memorable example of negative capability.
5 Paz, Octavio
6 Joyce, James
7 Plath, Sylvia
8 Ibid
9 Sacks, Oliver *The Mind's Eye*

WORKS CITED AND CONSULTED

Blake, William. "Vison of the Daughter of Albion." *The Complete Poetry and Prose of William Blake*. Edited by David Erdman. University of California Press, 1982, p196.

Dickinson, Emily. Letter to T.W. Higginson, July 1862. *The Letters of Emily Dickinson*. Edited by Thomas H. Johnson. Belknap-Harvard University Press, 1986, p. 411.

Eide, Brock L. and Fernette F. *The Dyslexic Advantage: Unlocking the Hidden Potential of the Dyslexic Brain*. Penguin-Plume, 2011.

Falchuk, Brad. *The Yale Center for Dyslexia & Creativity Newsletter*, September 2019, p.2.

Gass, William. "Representation and the War for Reality." Habitations of the Word. Cornell University Press, 1985, p. 97.

Gruber. H. *Darwin on Man: A Psychological Study of Scientific Creativity. Together with Darwin's Early and Unpublished Notebooks*, transcribed and annotated by Paul H. Barrett. Wildwood House, 1974, p. 340.

Joyce, James. *Ulysses*. Vintage, 1990, p. 24.

Keats, John. February 19, 1818, *Letters of John Keats*. Editor Robert Gittings. Oxford University Press, 1970.

—. "Ode to a Nightingale." Poetry Foundation. https://www.poetryfoundation.org/poems/44479/ode-to-a-nightingale Accessed 24 April 2013.

Lingis, Alphonso. "Animal Body, Inhuman Face." *Zootologies: The Question of the Animal*. Edited by Cary Wolfe. University of Minnesota Press, 2003, p. 181.

Matisse, Henri. Quoted in Charles Riley. *Color Codes: Modern Theories of Color in Philosophy, Painting and Architecture, Literature, Music, and Psychology*. University Press of New England, 1995, p.124.

Paz, Octavio. "Before Sleep." *Eagle or Sun?* Translated by Eliot Weinberger. New Directions Press, 1976, p. 6.

Pessoa, Fernando. *Book of Disquiet.* Translated by Richard Zenith. Penguin Books, 2002, p.350.

Plath, Sylvia. "Poppies in July." *The Collected Poems.* Edited by Ted Hughes. New York: Harper-Perennial, 1981, p. 203.

PolitiFact.com. "Cannon Gets Connection Between Reading and Crime Right."<http://www.politifact.com/oregon/statements/2012/feb/13/ben-cannon/canon-gets-connection-between-reading-and-crime-ri/> Accessed 23 May 2014.

Polster, Arnim. "On the Use and Abuse of Reading: Karl Philipp Moritz and the Dialectic of Pedagogy in Late-Enlightenment Germany." *Impure Reason: Dialectic of Enlightenment in Germany.* Edited by W. Daniel Wilson and Robert C. Holub. Wayne State University Press, 1993, p. 466.

Sacks, Oliver. *The Mind's Eye.* Vintage-Random House, 2011, p. 7.

Sebald, W.G. *Austerlitz.* Random House, 2001, p. 4.

Shaywitz, Sally. *Overcoming Dyslexia.* Knopf, 2012.

Stein, Gertrude. *Tender Buttons.* Sun and Moon Press, 1991, pp. 17, 11.

Waldrop, Rosmarie. *Reproduction of Profiles.* New Directions, 1987, pp. 9, 68.

Weil, Simone. "Essay on the Notion of Reading." Translated by Rebecca Fine Rose and Timothy Tessen. *Philosophical Investiation* 13:4, 1990, p. 36.

Wittgenstein, Ludwig. *Remarks on Color.* Edited by G.E.M. Anscombe. Translated by Linda L. McAlister and Margarete Schattle, Wiley-Blackwell, 1991, pp. 45, 55.

Wolf, Maryanne. *Proust and the Squid: The story and Science of the Reading Brain.* Harper-Perennial, 2008.